Adultery: 101 Reasons Why Not to Cheat

Paul Davis

Copyright © 2007 by Paul Davis

Adultery: 101 Reasons Not to Cheat
by Paul Davis

Printed in the United States of America

ISBN-13: 978-1-60034-853-2
ISBN-10: 1-60034-853-X

All rights reserved solely by the author. The author guarantees all contents are original and do not infringe upon the legal rights of any other person or work. No part of this book may be reproduced in any form without the permission of the author. The views expressed in this book are not necessarily those of the publisher.

Unless otherwise indicated, Bible quotations are taken from the King James Version from biblegateway.com.

www.xulonpress.com

Acknowledgments

Thanks to my wife Karla for helping me to stay sane in an insane world. Your love and faithful support strengthen me personally whereby I can have a strong foundation from which to impact the nations. Thanks for bringing a new world order to our house, whereby our home can be a place where heaven can come to earth.

Thanks to Pastors Carlos Sarmiento, Amar Rambisoon, and Mark Chironna for successfully modeling manhood and ministry. You have provided me a point of reference, prophetic insight, and hope for my own life. Indeed purity and passion is both possible and powerful.

Thanks to my mother and father, Paul and Paulette Davis, for their steadfast love through every season of my life. Your marriage of over thirty years has shown me what it is to rejoice and happily live together. Thanks for all your love and laughs we have shared together.

Table of Contents

Introduction ix

101 Reasons Not to Cheat 17

Prayer of Repentance and Restoration 75

Fear the Lord and Depart from Evil 81

Introduction

"A true man does not need to romance a different woman every night, a true man romances the same woman for the rest of her life."

As a woman you don't want a man to see you and think, "I want to spend the night with you." Live in such a way that a man says, "I want to spend my life with you."

Once having said, "I do" how can we obtain the blessings of matrimony and avoid adultery? Obtaining a spouse requires effort, as does maintaining a loving marriage. If we are not careful, we can at times begin to inwardly devalue the spouse God gave us. To not properly appreciate your God-given mate is to devalue the blessing of marriage.

"He who finds a wife finds a good thing and obtains favor from the Lord" (Proverbs 18:22). She who finds a loving husband has also found a good thing and would do well to honor him.

Nobody wants to be with a person who does not celebrate or desire them. When not properly and consistently attended to love can grow cold. Nevertheless this is no reason to let love die. Love can be renewed and strengthened if we hold to our marital covenant. As you endeavor to uphold your marital vows before God, expect divine intervention to help you.

Being an unappreciative spouse can lead to much pain and heartache. A root of bitterness can easily spring up in the marital relationship, as living within such close proximity with a person there are ample opportunities to be offended. Jesus said offenses will come. Woe to that person through whom they come (Matthew 18:7). Offense is the bait of Satan, which disconnects you from divine relationship and your heavenly purpose. Implosion, explosion and relational erosion can rapidly occur if the offense is not quickly dealt with.

Profanity and adultery are two of the many responses of a person who has become bitter. Esau was bitter toward Jacob and despised his very birthright, which he exchanged for a bowl of stew when he was hungry (Genesis 25:29-34). By the time Esau came to the point of properly valuing his birthright, it was too late. Esau's inheritance was lost, though he sought it with tears. No place of repentance was given Esau, neither was he accepted (Hebrews 12:16-17; Malachi 1:3).

Many are they who have been on their knees with tears in their eyes begging their spouse to stay. Likewise many are they who have strayed in adulterous affairs only to wake up weeks later and find they have lost everything.

Lust is not love. Infatuation is a deadly attraction. Sin is the blast that doesn't last. It is a poison pill that will taste good for a while but turn toxic in your belly.

When you disregard your marital vows, covenant and promises you despise your own self-worth. Your word is your worth. Without personal worth and self-esteem nobody can make you feel good about yourself. Run to as many lovers as you will, but you still will feel ill. Self-respect must be earned. It cannot be gained by fleshly gratification. That only diminishes your self-worth and plunges you into the pit of hell.

God however wants to lift you up and out of that state of mind. The Lord of glory wants to renew your mind and transform your life. The Matchmaker above also wants to preserve your marriage. The Creator of heaven and earth is fighting for your marriage.

Don't distort and run from the truth. Embrace and acknowledge the truth so you can be free! Freedom feels good! Doing right feels good. You sleep better at night when you do right. You feel better about yourself when you look into the mirror. Your heart is pure and joyful when live right.

It's hard to go wrong when you do right. Don't be out alone late. Go home! Don't travel alone. Guard your heart. Fight for your marriage. Covenantal love is wonderful and enduring. A one-night stand is a lie, which you should not buy. Adultery is a gross sin you will surely pay for. Don't subject yourself to such suffering.

Good understanding gives favor: but the way of transgressors is hard (Proverbs 13:15). Most people never sin alone. Transgressors always want to drag somebody else with them into their sin. Misery loves company. Guilty consciences don't sit well alone. They want to bring you home.

Don't entertain transgressors who intend only to lead you along with them. The integrity of the upright shall guide them: but the perverseness of transgressors shall destroy them (Proverbs 11:3). Stay away from transgressors who think to lead you astray and destroy your marriage. Show me your friends and I will show you your future.

If your friends talk bad about and don't respect your spouse, don't associate with them. Anybody who encourages you to cheat on your spouse is not your friend. They are the friend and messenger of Satan, sent to destroy your marriage and life.

The righteousness of the upright shall deliver them: but transgressors shall be taken in their own naughtiness (Proverbs 11:6). Transgressors know the truth, but do otherwise. Their own rebellion shall punish them.

God is a good God. Our Creator is trying to get blessings and good things to us. That is why His Word gives us commandments to protect and preserve us from destruction. Self-willed disobedience will surely destroy you and curse your family too.

The eyes of the LORD preserve knowledge, and He overthrows the words of the transgressor (Proverbs 22:12). Don't trust in a person's words if their actions don't line up. You will know a tree by its fruit, not its talk. Observe a person's walk more than what you hear from their talk.

A whore is a deep ditch; and a strange woman is a narrow pit. She also lies in wait as for a prey, and increases the transgressors among men (Proverbs 23:27-28). Beware of wild women who sleep with every Tom, Dick and Harry. You think you are going to play, but to her you are her prey. She and her father the devil are seeking to destroy your life.

The great God that formed all things both rewards the fool, and rewards transgressors (Proverbs 26:10). Don't be deceived. God is not mocked. You surely will reap what you sow (Galatians 6:7).

Sowing your time into adultery and prostitution means reaping sorrow and destruction. Wake up before it's too late! Harness your flesh with a vengeance. Get an accountability partner with all diligence. Practice self-control and prudence. Spend extra time in prayer, fasting and God's Presence to overcome the flesh.

If you don't, you will soon be devastated by your own fleshly lusts. Being bowed down on the floor with eyes full of tears, hugging your spouse's ankles and pleading with them to stay while they walk out the door is not fun.

Choose instead a better way. Cultivate your marital relationship daily and properly esteem your spouse. Keep them close by your side. Whenever you are apart (even if just for a few hours) maintain a good attitude and right mindset toward your spouse.

Don't entertain sexist conversations and spouse degrading comments. When you give ear to people who belittle and downgrade your spouse, you are saying that you approve of it. What you tolerate will eventually dominate. Whatever you do not resist, will surely persist.

Such attitudes and sinful tendencies in thought, word and deed precede the act of adultery. God wants to preserve marriages and secure for you meaningful relationship. Your Creator has your best interest at heart.

Your unruly flesh is crazy and only wants immediate gratification – food, sleep and sex. You therefore must renew your mind, strengthen your spirit and harness your flesh. If you don't you soon may be the enemy's next target and victim. Don't be another casualty of infidelity and divorce.

Rise up with a renewed purpose and divine force to nullify the attacks of the enemy. Be all you can be! Fight to preserve your personal and marital purity.

This book is spiritual food, a weapon with which to war against the enemy, and a treasure to prepare your heart for both matrimony and eternity. Your marriage can be heaven on earth!

Adultery is a disguised detour en route to your personal demise. Don't travel down that dead end street. Read this book and be armed for battle to overcome Delilah and Jezebel when they show up in your life. Women beware of Amnon who will patronize you to get in your pants after which he will hate and betray you.

I have written this book for myself, my wife, and anybody desiring to be or stay married. The Bible exhorts us to be "sober minded." This book will sober you up in regard to the blessing of marriage and cause you to want to fight to maintain the marvelous marital relationship.

Praise ye the LORD. Blessed is the man that fears the Lord, that delights greatly in His commandments (Psalm 112:1).

He will bless them that fear the Lord, both small and great (Psalm 115:13).

Now, let's get started.

Here are 101 reasons to be faithful to your spouse and not cheat!

1. You might get dismembered.

Jesus said if a member of your body offends you by causing you to habitually sin, "cut it off" (Matt.5:30). John Bobbit's wife did it for him, cutting his penis off when he cheated on her. That serves as a reminder that when you're a bad boy, the bad girl in your wife might just come to the forefront and repay you.

I heard one fellow minister say to another minister: "He won't cheat on his wife. If he were to cheat on her, she'd cut out his kidney or something."

Such vengeance and violence is commonplace in our society, so let's not slip up and provoke our spouse unnecessarily! We can use some more fear of God and the repercussions for wrong doing in our nation.

2. Those who commit adultery are often murdered.

Jealousy is the rage of a man: therefore he will not spare in the day of vengeance (Proverbs 6:34-35). Adultery leads to intense rage, vengeance and judgment. Prepare yourself for the consequences and repercussions if you indulge in it.

3. Your sin will find you out, after which it will be told and noised abroad.

Samson went to Gaza, saw a harlot and went in unto her. And it was told (Judg.16:1-2). For there is nothing hid, which shall not be manifested (Mark 4:22). Make no mistake about it. Your sin will find you out (Numbers 32:23). People talk.

4. Monica Lewinsky turned on President Clinton after they did the nasty.

What juicy tidbits of information will come to the light about you after you are done getting some? Think about that sticky jam, when it all finally hits the fan!

If she or he with whom you're committing adultery is that easy, you've got no guarantee of them being there with you tomorrow. People who strip down and get naked with you easily aren't the ideal people with whom to associate. Being given to their fluctuating feelings they are unpredictable. As quickly as they came into your life they can likewise soon leave, after which they very well might turn on you. Then you will be left to your own demise. Hence wake up and realize the error of your ways. Catch yourself before you slip up and heavily pay! Don't dance if you're not prepared to pay the fiddler.

5. Sexually transmitted diseases are the reward of adultery.

Today a quick thrill can lead to a big hospital bill. Wild gratuitous sex can produce diseases that torment and vex. Once you contract the AIDs virus it is yours forever. Therefore count the cost before you give unbridled sex much thought.

Sexually transmitted diseases (STDs) remain a major public health challenge in the United States. While substantial progress has been made in preventing, diagnosing, and treating certain STDs in recent years, the Center for Disease Control estimates that 19 million new infections occur each year, almost half of them among young people ages 15 to 24. In addition to the physical and psychological consequences of STDs, these diseases also exact a tremendous economic toll. Direct medical costs associated with STDs in the United States are estimated at $13 billion annually.

This document summarizes 2004 national data on trends in notifiable STDs — chlamydia, gonorrhea, and syphilis — that are published in CDC's report, *Sexually Transmitted Disease Surveillance 2004* (available at www.CDC.gov/STD/stats). These data, which are useful for examining overall trends and trends among populations at risk, represent only a small proportion of the true national burden of STDs. Many cases of notifiable STDs go undiagnosed, and some highly prevalent viral infections, such as human papillomavirus and genital herpes, are not reported at all.

Magic Johnson, former MBA all-star, contracted AIDs when cheating on his wife. So don't think you are exempt from getting sexually transmitted diseases.

6. Feelings fluctuate and change.
Sleep on it and wait on the Lord, an hour or day, after which you may not want to cheat on your spouse. Let patience have its perfect work (James 1:4).

7. Adultery will cause you to have split personalities, multiple identities, and to become a people-pleasing chameleon.
Your ability to stand for truth and your own convictions will deteriorate and disintegrate as you first try to protect your character from being maligned and assassinated. The irony is you will have already destroyed yourself from within, so you will excessively seek to sustain yourself outwardly following the adultery. You may effectively be able to lie to and fool others, but you cannot lie to yourself. All of your conflicting scripts as to who you are will surely greatly divide your identity and cause you to question yourself.

8. The level of trust others put in you will be greatly diminished if not forever ruined.
Your wife, family, friends and co-workers follow you because of trust – trust in your integrity. Image is

what people think we are. Integrity is what we really are, without which trust will be nonexistent.

Your word will not mean anything anymore. Once you have said "I do" and don't, everyone will know it and hesitate to take you at your word. People want to see your walk match your talk. Lip service alone will not satisfy as talk is cheap. Commitment endures circumstantial challenges and holds true to one's word regardless of external factors.

9. Fear of getting caught torments the soul.

Having to walk around on egg-shells and always cover your tracks is not a healthy way to live. Fear carries with it great torment. Why afflict such lasting pain upon your soul for a brief physical experience? The severity of mental anguish and reoccurring stress caused to the mind is not worth whatever fleshly pleasure is temporarily gained.

10. You will continually have to lie to cover your tracks.

Lies tend to give birth to more lies. One lie opens the door for more questions to come your way regarding the sequence of events, which in turn demands that you either fess up with the truth or keep on covering your tracks with perpetual lies. Liars have no home in heaven, but rather in hell with the father of lies the devil (John 8:44; Revelation 21:8).

11. Adultery troubles the heart and mind.

Live with a pure heart. Blessed are the pure in heart because they shall see God (Matthew 5:8). Such people can be transparent, real and open about their struggles because they are sincerely trying to keep themselves pure and not give into temptation. Temptations come upon us all, but we don't have to yield to them. Purity is more easily achieved when you associate with pure hearted people. A pure and childlike heart is a tremendous blessing.

There is no peace for the adulterer. There is no peace to the wicked (Isaiah 57:21). Peace is a fruit of God's Spirit that must be cultivated, possessed and bore (Galatians 5:22-23). Jesus the Prince of peace gives us peace like a river when we wait upon Him (Isaiah 66:12), even a peace that surpasses understanding (Philippians 4:7). Once you've got God's peace, fight off restlessness to keep it. Patiently possess your soul and be made whole (Lk.21:19). God gives perfect peace to them whose mind is stayed upon Him (Isaiah 26:3). Run from adultery and possess peace of mind and conscience.

Sex without commitment works havoc to your soul. The harlot seeks for the precious life of a man (Proverbs 6:26). Upon getting it she casts down his might and leaves him wounded. Her house is the way to hell, going down to the chambers of death (7:27). To entertain the adulteress is to decline in heart and set your self up to be wounded (v. 24-27). "Whosoever commits adultery with a woman lacks understanding: he that does it destroys his own soul" (6:32).

12. Your children will suffer significantly.

It is a known fact that children without a solid family unit established within their home often tend to be soulishly lacking in some capacity and socially challenged. Because God wants a godly seed, he warns men not to deal treacherously with their wives (Malachi 2:15). Preserve the marital union for the well being of your children.

13. You will be marked by dishonor and the reproach will not be wiped away.

He that commits adultery will get a wound and dishonor; and his reproach shall not be wiped away (Proverbs 6:32-33). Consider basketball star Kobe Bryant. His sexual fling came back to sting. He was smeared across newspapers for his infidelity.

Cheating destroys your honor and personal dignity. A good name is a valuable possession, more valuable than riches. Infidelity however ruins one's personal honor and dignity. "Whosoever commits adultery . . . destroys his own soul

When high profile people commit adultery, they often try to pay off the person to keep their mouth shut. The giving of gifts however won't buy back your integrity neither will it redeem your reputable name (Proverbs 6:35).

Your reputation and name will lose its credibility in the community. Nobody wants to be doing business or covenanting in relationship with a covenant breaker. Such a person has not retained God in their knowledge and therefore has been given over by God Himself to a reprobate mind (Romans 1:28). What you say therefore has no credibility and cannot be trusted since you break covenants as easily as you make them.

A good name is rather to be chosen than great riches, and loving favor rather than silver and gold (Proverbs 22:1). A good name will take you further in life than monetary substance. Your reputation and name is more marketable than the money you possess. Your credibility is not determined by your wealth but by your name.

14. Your life will be out of balance, not gel and flow.

Like a disjointed skeleton or puzzle missing pieces, you will be out of sorts apart from your Creator. When you get married, you become one. Removing that special one from your life whom you are a part of removes something from you.

Beyond what others think of you is what you think of you. You may be able to fool others, but you cannot lie to yourself. Unconscious incompetence can only last so long until the wake-up call comes blaring through. God knows how to get your attention. Eventually the mirror of the Word of God will be put in front of your face so you can see yourself as you truly are. Why not take a look now therefore into the Word, ways, and will of God?

It is better to fall upon the rock and be broken, than to have the rock fall upon you and crush you to powder (Matthew 21:44). Get your life back in order and stop running from the truth.

15. Your life's legacy will be tattered and torn.

"A good man leaves an inheritance to his children's children: and the wealth of the sinner is laid up for the just" (Proverbs 13:22). Cheating on your spouse will cause your good name to be lost and therefore your children will have to answer for your sins (Exodus 20:5). A good name is the best thing you can leave for your children.

16. You reap what you sow.

Can you stomach the thought of your wife in the arms of another man? Disobedience to God results in you betrothing a wife and another man lying with her (Deuteronomy 28:30). David committed adultery and in return got the same in an even worse fashion. What David did in secret with Bathsheba, his son Absalom did to his concubines in broad daylight (2 Samuel 12:11-12; 16:21-22).

When you cheat on your spouse, you enrage them with malice to do the same to you but worse. Unless you want the ante raised on you don't cheat.

17. Variety carries the scent of death.

Why go hunting female flesh when you can be satisfied with the wife of your youth at home? What it will take much effort to get beyond the borders of your marriage, you can readily and easily get from your wife without a huge expenditure of time and money – because you've already made that investment.

Be blessed and rejoice with the wife of your youth. Be satisfied always with her breasts; and be ravished always with her love (Proverbs 5:18-19).

Variety is not the spice of life. It carries the scent of death in regard to marriage. If you have a good thing at home don't be so quick to roam. Be thankful and rejoice in your spouse!

You never know how good it is until you discover how bad it can become. Cheating on your spouse is dumb.

18. Cheating on your spouse is a waste of money.

When you play around with multiple sex partners you devastate yourself financially. "By means of a whorish woman a man is brought to a piece of bread: and the adulteress will hunt for the precious life." (Proverbs 6:26)

Adultery causes you to squander your life on meaningless things as you waste your God given talents, abilities, and resources. At the end of your life you will wake up and realize that you have squandered your precious life on meaningless things that never satisfy. In that day you will cry, "How have I hated instruction, and my heart despised reproof; and have not obeyed the voice of my teachers, nor inclined mine ear to them that instructed me!" (Proverbs 5:11-13; 18:9) Destruction shall be to the workers of iniquity (21:15). Hell and destruction are never full; so the eyes of man are never satisfied (27:20).

Millions of dollars are wasted every year on adulteress affairs that rob families of finances. Invest in your marriage and children's future. Don't squander your family's hard earned money on cheap sex that doesn't fulfill.

19. Adultery is a waste of time.

We must redeem the time because the days in which we live are evil (Ephesians 5:16).

Our times are in God's hand. No man knows the duration of his life, neither the day which he shall expire from the earth. The way we live before God will determine what expiration date He gives us. They that are serving God and planted in His house will bring forth fruit in old age (Psalm 92:14). They who love and live for God will be satisfied with long life.

"Because he has set his love upon Me [God] . . . with long life will I satisfy him, and show him My salvation" (Psalm 91:14-16).

Whoremongers and adulterers however God will judge (Hebrews 13:4). The judgment of God can cut your life off in an instant. We must remember it is God who gives us the breath we breathe (Acts 17:27-28).

20. Cheating is too much work for too little enjoyment.

Building a whole new relationship is a lot of work. Having to introduce yourself to a new person and getting acquainted can be time consuming. It is far better to cultivate the marital relationship you already have. An orgasm only lasts a short time.

Therefore don't waste precious time on a prostitute or adulteress.

Marital history is a wonderful thing as with it comes extensive relatability and memories. Considering the amount of time and money you have already invested in your marriage, why should you begin all over again and have to reinvest afresh in a new relationship? All relationships have bumps in the road and knocks that occur along the way.

It's like driving a car down a street. Some streets are better than others. Yet these things are often unavoidable and part and parcel of the marital package. Don't run from them and think to work at another new relationship when you are unwilling to work on the relationship beneath your feet.

There is way too much effort and mental exertion involved in going through the getting acquainted stage all over again when you've already got it going on. Just believe and receive.

21. The family will be hurt and torn.

Establishing cordial and good working relationships among in laws in the extended family can take time. Once relational rhythm is established, a marital divorce can cause each to feel uncomfortable with the other and the extended family. This is very unfair to the parents from both sides, who so generously and lovingly supported each of you while you were married.

Cheating on your spouse can immediately ruin those marvelous relationships that took time and toil to build. Consider your in laws as your immediate family and know that any ungodly decision you make will adversely effect them and not just yourself. Walk in love and crucify your selfishness that would cause you to hurt your family.

Hurt people hurt people. Rest assured that if you begin breaking hearts, what you sow you will soon reap (Galatians 6:7). Infidelity breaks hearts and spreads outward. Be careful. Things dear to your heart will be trampled upon in the process. Those you hurt will carry bitterness and thus communicate and spread that to others, causing a multiplying affect. Inconsideration breeds more inconsideration. The human heart is a fragile thing not to be trampled upon. Roots of bitterness multiply.

"Looking diligently lest any man fail of the grace of God; lest any root of bitterness springing up trouble you, and thereby many be defiled" (Hebrews 12:15). Your family's hurt will express itself through anger. Once anger has festered you will be despised by family for your unfaithfulness.

When you break the covenantal vows of holy matrimony, your relatives and friends are going to talk about you. They may not say it to your face, but rest assured their regard for you will be adversely affected. Some will utterly despise you for your ungodly and immoral actions. No amount of excuses and justifications will make amends and change their opinion of you afterward.

22. Cheating causes countless losses.

It takes a lifetime to build a successful marriage and family. Yet it takes only a minute to lose it all. A few minutes of careless behavior can cause all you worked so hard to obtain to come tumbling down like Humpty Dumpty in a moment.

Consider the tangible and intangible blessings of marriage, the family, and having a home before you throw it all to the wind. Many who rejoiced in an affair temporarily mourned in the end when their flesh and body were consumed. One cried out saying: "How have I hated instruction, and my heart despised reproof" (Prov.5:11-12).

It takes a lot to attract a holy God to you and bring His awesome mighty anointing upon your life. Yet it takes very little sin to pollute your heart and cause the Holy Spirit to leave you. Ask Samson. He knows the pain of impurity with which he was enslaved and made blind (Judges 16).

And she said, "The Philistines *are* upon you, Samson!" So he awoke from his sleep, and said, "I will go out as before, at other times, and shake myself free!" But he did not know that the Lord had departed from him (Judges 16:20).

Delilah, the very woman that whispered sweet nothings in Samson's ear, was the same woman who announced the arrival of his enemies.

23. Looks are deceiving as is cheating.

Just because a fleshpot looks good does not mean they are good. Many people within minutes of opening their mouth convey their true inner nature. Upon discovering just who that person really is you may not want to be with them after all. Once it has been revealed that the person who you are so attracted to lacks any character and are soulishly shallow – you may not want to be with them as much as you thought. "Beauty is vain" (Proverbs 31:30).

One southern preacher got married to a beautiful woman with a lovely voice. On their wedding night before going to bed, she took off her eyelashes, removed her wig, and placed her false teeth in the bathroom. Upon seeing all of this, the preacher cried out: "Sing woman! Sing!"

Better than love at first sight, is love with divine insight. Many women dress seductively because they realize they have nothing else with which to attract and keep a man.

24. The grass is not likely to be any greener on the other side.

People always dress themselves up at the beginning, but when you get close enough you realize they too have issues and peculiarities you may not like. God made you a triune being – spirit, mind and body – which is to say the flesh alone will not fulfill you. A new and improved model in the flesh so to say will not guarantee you inner happiness.

Before you partake of the goods and lose your marriage, consider that you are a triune being that requires more than neighing. Bridle your passions and protect your marriage. Trust your instincts in that you chose to marry that person for a reason. Relive and rediscover what attracted you to your spouse in the first place. Remember what drew you to them and made you say "I do." Reassess their attributes and valuable qualities before getting your head stuck in a barbed wire fence looking elsewhere.

25. A picture is often better than the real thing.

People can hide stuff and masquerade themselves in pictures. It is not a funny thing at all, but nonetheless it is quite true. It is no different in real life. It takes a long time to truly get to know a person. Don't believe everything you see and hear upon first glance.

Hotels and resorts when advertising their facility tend to take the photograph from the best possible angle so as to emphasize their strengths and diminish their weaknesses. That is to say if a hotel is poorly situated next to a major highway, you can rest assured that the photo promoting their hotel won't reveal that noisy intersection next to it.

The same goes with people. A man or woman might have the most attractive face (for those of you shopping on the internet), but not disclose by photograph that they are one-hundred pounds overweight. Photographs are not grumpy nor do they nag.

Things at a distance can be hidden which once you are up and close tend to be revealed. If love is a dream, marriage is the alarm clock. Wake up and realize that whoever you get close enough to will also have flaws. While considering flaws, consider your own and stay home.

26. Cheating affects your relationship with God and His people.

Messing around on your spouse will cause your God given relationships in the house of the Lord to be severed as distrust and uncertainty can spread. Once the seed of disloyalty is sown a harvest of distrust is reaped. We must therefore fight to maintain godly relationships, which have divine input to deposit into our lives.

None of us are as strong as all of us. We all have blind spots. The Church of God is there to help strengthen your marriage and family. Take off the mask and get help when you need it. God gives grace to the humble. Don't worry about those who may accuse and criticize. Get help and your marriage will be fortified.

27. Going through the dating and matrimony process again can be laborious and agonizing.

Some years ago while working at the Hyatt hotel, I witnessed a singles event. The majority of those in attendance were middle age and up. Altogether they were a quite heavy-hearted bunch despite their professional occupations which they seemingly flaunted so as to put their best foot forward.

After the evening event one lady left the hotel and proceeded to get her car from the valet. I heard her say to herself in passing upon exiting the hotel: "I should never have divorced my husband."

The disgust and heartbreak with which she said those words stuck with me. The bottom line is finding a suitable partner for life can be quite laborious and agonizing. If you had enough confidence to marry the person you are with, why not endure the storms of life and stay with them.

My father gave me some wise counsel regarding marriage saying: "If you hang in there it only gets better." As all marriages do, my dad and step-mom went through some bumps in the marital road. Yet they hung in there and endured. My brother and I are most glad they did. Today they have a wonderful marriage and are a tremendous example to newly-weds and veterans alike. They are best friends and lovers whom I love dearly.

28. It is not good to be alone.

Just because you've got someone to sleep with you does not eliminate the problem of loneliness. Loneliness is not necessarily the absence of people. It is the absence of people who understand and connect with you. The adulterer will sleep with you, after which he will move on leaving you alone to yourself.

In the beginning God said, "It's not good for man to be alone." (Genesis 2:18)

Now if the manufacturer said this concerning the human race, we then ought to take heed. Of course this does not apply to everyone, but if you are married it applies to you. If you felt compelled to marry due to loneliness or compulsion, you have no right to sever the marital bond once you've entered into this sacred covenant.

God has now entered this union with you and a threefold cord has been tied (Ecclesiastes 4:12). It is not you and your spouse in this thing alone. No! God Himself is a part of this marital union. So before going to some negative "friend" who would counsel you to divorce, you had better go to God and have discourse.

29. Sex is not love. Adultery therefore won't carry the emotional stimulation nor the feelings found in love.

Men need sex. Yes, women do too, but the sexual drive in men tends to outweigh that of women due to higher testosterone levels.

One Saturday Night Live episode portrayed this when some women huddled amongst themselves were sighing with disgusted looks on their faces saying, "Thanks Viagra." In other words, we were quite happy with our husband's impotence or infrequency before the new wonder drug was discovered and now we're wore out with the excessive sexual activity that it has resurrected in our husbands.

It cannot be overemphasized that sex is not love. Men typically give intimacy to get sex. Women on the other hand often barter with sex in an attempt to get intimacy. Until both sexes determine the needs of the other and in love freely give without strings or remorse, than love will not reign supreme in the marital relationship. When love takes preeminence and sex takes the backseat, more sexual activity will likely result as love will seek to utilize all forms of communication to express itself.

Prostitutes give sex, but rarely are they taken home to stay. That's why these peddlers of sex on the street look so haggard and abused. This further indicates that sex does not provide the utmost fulfillment in life. For if it did these who hire prostitutes would take them home to stay.

As for prostitutes, the movie *Pretty Woman* showed how they rarely kiss their clients as true love is nonexistent and therefore they provide sex in a very functional manner rather than with all the affectionate expressions of love that typically precede sex in a marital relationship.

As one man put it: "Having sex with a prostitute was like having sex with a robot or machine, no emotional feeling whatsoever. I'm going home to my wife."

30. Immediate gratification apart from commitment results in eventual disappointment.

What you don't commit to you cannot expect commitment from. Marriage provides relational commitment, which is very reassuring and settling to the soul. People like roots. They don't like to be continually uprooted and transplanted. Too many relationships entering and leaving your life can be like adverse winds blowing against you.

What you can immediately get, you tend to not be grateful for. What you have to cultivate and work hard for, you tend to value and cherish. This is the difference between being kinky and being committed. The former has no promise of longevity or consistency. The latter promises both and much more!

In Egypt during the days of Moses, the darkness was so dark it could be felt (Exodus 10:21). Sin and its darkness can also be felt. It's like eating cotton candy. It never quite fills or satisfies you.

31. You will lose all of your marital history you've worked hard to build.

Your marriage is a part of your life's history, something you've been gradually building day by day. To throw it all away is to discard a part of your life and piece of your soul.

Memories cannot be relived once elderly relatives have gone on, children have grown up and experiences past. That is they cannot be relived unless you have a person with whom you shared those relationships and experiences. If you mess up and divorce that person, you throw away many fond and wonderful memories along with them.

32. Disobedience to God works disaster.

He that sins against God robs his own soul (Proverbs 8:36). To resist and hate God is to love death. Our God is not a mean, heartless judge issuing out commands without first having taken your interest to heart. God is not some police man in the sky issuing out citations.

God's commands are given because of His great love with which He loves us and thereby fosters our best interests. Disobedience to God brings harm to our lives as we step out from under His mighty hand of protection and open ourselves up to demonic attack.

More than God endeavoring to punish us is the element of self-destruction wherewith our denial of truth and blatant rebellion brings unnecessary hardship upon us. Curses are the end result of disobedience to God (Deuteronomy 28:15-68).

Learn from David, a man after God's own heart, who also committed adultery. David said, "My flesh trembles for fear of You; and I am afraid of Your judgments" (Ps.119:120).

33. Cheating causes you to miss the wonderful plan of God for your life.

Your life is a portrait being painted continuously by God as you remain on His easel. When you bolt and go your own way, you disrupt the portrait God is endeavoring to paint.

"Eye has not seen, nor ear heard, neither has it entered into the heart of man, the things which God has prepared for them that love Him" (1 Corinthians 2:9). In other words, God has better things for those who wait upon Him and live within the perimeters He has set for us (Hebrews 6:9).

34. Adultery leaves you to always live with regret.

Sitting alone wondering what could have been, what should have been, and what might have been is very painful. The agony that comes with second guessing yourself and reverting back to your old manner of life, once you have tasted the heavenly gift in Christ, is torturous to the soul.

It is far better to live out the course of your life under God's hand and keep your vows so you can fully prove God and His Word. Esau despised his birthright and therefore lost it forever. By the time Esau realized the value of that which he had lost, it was too late. Though he sought it with tears, it was gone and unattainable (Hebrews 12:16-17).

35. Your selfishness will eventually catch up with you.

Give and it will come back to you (Luke 6:38). Be stingy and withhold your hand and a curse shall come upon you (Proverbs 11:26; 28:27). The law of reciprocity is sure to come back to bless or haunt you.

What comes around goes around. Sin is selfish. Jesus instituted what is now known as the golden rule, which says "Do unto others as you'd have them do unto you" (Luke 6:31).

A self-centered life will leave you feeling insignificant and unable to measure up. When Adam took his eyes off of God and positioned them upon himself, his inadequacy surfaced and caused him to go into hiding (Genesis 3:8-11).

36. Adultery causes your head to hang low in depression.

You won't be able to proudly look at yourself in the mirror. God is the glory and the lifter of your head (Psalm 3:3). Sin causes your head to hang low in shame. The wicked flee at the presence of the righteous (Proverbs 28:1). Righteousness provides inner security and causes you to be bold.

Something erodes within when the contaminants of sin adversely affect the inward parts. Sin is detrimental to one's self image and personal posture. There can be no true feeling of self-confidence when sin has brought instability within. David therefore prayed to God asking him for "truth in the inward parts" as his bones suffered under the weight of his sin (Psalm 51:6, 8).

Depression will linger at times and seek to forever demoralize you. Depression is a deadly disease of the soul taking you down to the depths of despair en route to hell itself. Your life partner who in the past picked you up and provided encouragement through life's lows will no more be there to lift you. Alone due to your adultery you will be demoralized.

37. Double mindedness works instability.

A double-minded man is unstable in all his ways (James 1:8). When your heart and mind are so divided as to whom you are to love or how many you are to divide your love between, you become emotionally incompetent. Incompetence in one area of life seems to eventually overflow into other areas of life. It therefore behooves us to be on our guard against diverse affections and the danger of allowing our soul to be sliced and segmented into pieces.

38. When you get what you want, you may not want what you've got.

Unbridled lust will take you further than you want to go, keep you longer than you want to stay, and cost you more than want to pay. To enter into God's rest we must be harnessed and inwardly develop contentment within, which in effect will enable us to remain focused on our God given assignment.

39. Refusing to be settled opens the door for restlessness and turmoil in every area of your life.

Restlessness leads to haste and unwise decisions. Frivolous behavior taken in a time of inner restlessness can cause much stress and strain in the long run because of unwise and detrimental decisions made in an hour of inner turmoil.

When in a state of inner turmoil and dissatisfaction, resist the urge to hastily move and run into something unhealthy. Instead step back and reevaluate. Pray. Get God's guidance. Ponder the path of your feet. Then move according to the will of God and the wisdom of His Spirit.

Societal restlessness must be resisted and divine contentment embraced so your soul can be settled and whole. Get a grip on yourself and settle down.

40. Adultery breaks your marital covenant before man and God.

Breaking covenant with God weakens your inner ability and confidence to keep covenant with man. Severing a divine covenant with Almighty God brings a curse upon you wherewith your ability to believe in yourself, your word, and your agreements to others is greatly diminished. It actually lessens the spirit of faith in your life. Without the spirit of faith your ability to believe and achieve is greatly undermined. The force of faith is entirely based upon your belief of the Word and your word included, without which you are greatly handicapped and so are those aligned with you.

God hates divorce. Divorce is man's creation, not God's. God is a covenant maker. Man is a covenant breaker. When man is redeemed in Christ and made to be Godlike by being led by His Spirit and directed by His Word, covenant keeping becomes second nature. The keeping of covenant is vital because it assures us of our future, settles our soul, increases our faith, and gives us boundaries within which to function.

When we are bad boys and girls, God does not deny Himself and break covenant with us. God is bound by His Word. Though we may deny Him, He shall never deny us. This is the essence of covenant – being bound to your word regardless of circumstances that would seemingly dictate otherwise. As God's children it brings much security to know that come hell or high water, God will be faithful to us. Our children born of our own flesh and blood need to know the same.

God hates divorce because He's concerned about our children. Our Creator wants a godly seed to be raised up in the earth. Only as our children behold a marital covenant kept in tact and daily walked out in strength and holiness before their eyes can they in turn desire God who keeps covenant for thousands of generations. Children who come from divorced families often have inner heart issues that makes it difficult for them (though not impossible) to draw near to God.

We must let God be true and every other man a liar. We must also be true to our own word lest we have the reputation of a liar ourselves. Nations that don't keep covenant and break their word have poor economies because they are not trusted. Living outside of your covenantal commitment breeds distrust and low self-esteem. After all, if others cannot trust you, what makes you think you can trust you? Being a covenant breaker erodes your own self-esteem and leaves you listless within. Be true to yourself, your word, your mate, and your God.

41. Your sweet sleep will be robbed from you as you prowl and stalk women in the late night hours.

Apart from your spouse you will grope in the darkness, as disobedience to God removes you from the light of His countenance. Never content and settled, you shall always be lusting for more, for another, for something more exciting. Yet inwardly you shall never be fulfilled. All the while gross darkness will increasingly permeate and fill your soul until you utterly loathe yourself. You will toss and turn at night. Unable to rest you will arise and go after your prey again.

Upon securing your next victim, you shall feast in fleshly delight. Yet at the end of your consumption, you shall remain dissatisfied and empty. Why? Because your outlook on life is determined by your inward look concerning yourself. It is your poor self-image and personal disgust of self that drives you to get the approval of other sex partners. Ironically however it is not their acknowledgment that you need as much as an understanding of what God says about you.

Unaware of what you truly want and need, you like a hunter continually pursue your prey. As you do you lose sleep and throw yourself deeper into dispair and continually rob from yourself your waking hours, minimizing your daily productivity, and plunging yourself into depravity. Like a dog in heat without control of your own fleshly lusts and cravings you'll be beat.

42. Adultery opens you up to demonic attack.

Satanic assaults are easy when you walk out from underneath God's hand of protection. Job was easily devoured by Satan once the hand of God's protection was removed. If Job, a man of God, could be annihilated by Lucifer what makes you think you are immune from Satanic assault?

Once you've tasted the heavenly gift and walk away you'll get seven times as many demon spirits to inhabit you (Matthew 12:43-45).

The favor of God will go from you and you'll be left to your own demise. God's favor is like dew on the early morning grass. God's favor is like icing on the cake. God's favor is like a beautiful sunrise that begins the day. God's favor rests upon His obedient children who worship and serve Him. Without God's favor you are left to yourself. Alone you must work in your own strength, toil with your own wisdom, and build with your own social connections.

Leaving your spouse and the God you committed to when you said to her, "I do." is a destructive thing. When you thrust God and your life partner from your side you bring upon yourself a certain judgment. God never intended for humans to be self-sufficient islands unto themselves. The favor of God is with His family, as is His favor upon His children who remain connected to His family. God's favor is a shield. God however is holy and cannot mix with your willful sin.

God hates feet that run to mischief (Proverbs 6:16-18). Therefore before you run straightway into the mouth of the devourer, think again. God who hates adultery and mischievous ways won't be swift to deliver you once you get yourself in that mess.

43. Secrecy and subtlety is Satanic.

"Stolen waters are sweet and bread eaten in secret is pleasant, but he does not know that the dead are there; and that her guests are in the depths of hell (Proverbs 9:17-18). "For it is a shame even to speak of those things which are done of them in secret" (Ephesians 5:12).

The slithery and slimy wiles of the devil will surely beguile and cover you with shame, after which you will have a grave among the dead. Rightfully so, because when you live a lie and resort to continual trickery you are dead within already. Live a life of righteousness so you don't have to slither around in secrecy like a snake.

44. You will have to live with condemnation and guilt.

Condemnation, guilt and shame are a heavy burden to bear. When we willfully sin against the Lord and our fellow man (in this instance our spouse) we bring upon ourselves a certain fearful judgment – an internal damnation of heart and mind. It happens when we come under the yoke of condemnation because we over-ride the inner conviction that comes by the Spirit to lead us out of temptation. Preferring the flesh over the Spirit, we find ourselves in sin giving into the appetites of the flesh. Sin having conceived then gives birth to death, inner and outer death.

Many are as if they were dead within, due to the weight of sin. Before choosing to feed the flesh, count the loss of soulish stability that will be incurred and the length of time that condemnation and guilt will have to be endured. The bodily lusts of the flesh are all the same, but the shame that comes with gratifying such lusts leave you inwardly bound and lame. Therefore get out of the sexual game and rest in Jesus Name.

45. Adultery is a seductive illusion through which your childlike heart and purity will be lost.

Sexual pleasures are readily available. Sex without God's peace and purity however is no blessing at all. The peace of God will only abound as you keep yourself within the borders of matrimony where true love is found. The innocence of a child can be had in a marital relationship where God is your Dad. Childlikeness not childishness, results in freedom of expression. Only the Spirit of God can remove inhibition and bring forth a pure exhibition of the Godhead. You owe it to yourself to be pure so that you can see God in every area of your life. Blessed are the pure in heart for they shall see God (Matthew 5:8).

That which you have in God is far better than anything the world can offer (Heb.6:9). Don't buy the lie. It's a mirage, an illusion. In actuality it is we in Christ who are most blessed and at rest. Yet the spirit of the age would have you to enter into restlessness and lose your contentment which is to go alongside your godliness.

It's interesting when the world is partying it up, they never show you the conclusion of the party at 2:00 or 3:00AM when the party is over and all the party animals aren't partying or celebrating anymore. They never show you who is the happiest come morning time. They never show you the world's kids hugging the toilet, smelling like a cigarette, or hungover in bed with a headache the next day. It's interesting how the media sells sin but never tells you the rest of the story and the consequences that follow right behind.

46. The innocence and faith you had in people will decrease, as you no longer can trust yourself.

To the pure all things are pure, but to the defiled and unbelieving is nothing pure; but even their mind and conscience is defiled (Titus 1:15). When you second-guess yourself, eventually you will begin to second-guess others. How you feel about yourself will effect what you project on to others. When self-trust diminishes, self-confidence declines right along with it.

47. You'll begin to see people as sex objects rather than humans created in God's image.

God created human beings in His image and likeness (Genesis 1:26). When you worship the creature more than the Creator, God turns you over to a reprobate mind (Romans 1:25, 28). Once your vile affections have taken over, all manner of uncleanness will occur and your body will be brought to dishonor being made susceptible to every evil illness (Romans 1:24).

48. Companionship will be lost.

Go from the presence of a foolish man, when you perceive not in him the lips of knowledge (Proverbs 14:7). People of substance and godly character will eventually realize your friendship is a liability not an asset. Be not deceived: evil communications corrupt good manners (1Corinthians 15:33). People of noble character will flee the presence of an immoral man.

49. Heavenly vision will be obscured.

Because you say, I am rich, and increased with goods, and have need of nothing; and know not that you are wretched, and miserable, and poor, and blind, and naked: I counsel you to buy of me gold tried in the fire, that you may be rich; and white raiment, that you may be clothed, and that the shame of your nakedness does not appear; and anoint your eyes with eye salve, that you may see (Revelation 3:17-18).

Self-indulgent living separates you from the heavenly vision, wherewith you cannot see the purpose of your life. It causes you to grope for the wall like the blind, and grope as if you had no eyes: you stumble at noon day as in the night; you are in desolate places as dead men (Isaiah 59:10).

50. Divine purpose and momentum will diminish.

And the kings of the earth, and the great men, and the rich men, and the chief captains, and the mighty men, and every bondman, and every free man, hid themselves in the dens and in the rocks of the mountains; and said to the mountains and rocks, "Fall on us, and hide us from the face of him that sits on the throne, and from the wrath of the Lamb" (Revelation 6:15-16).

You will loathe your own life and wish to die because your purpose has been lost. Elijah himself, a man of God, went a day's journey into the wilderness, and came and sat down under a juniper tree: and he requested for himself that he might die (1Kings 19:4).

How then will you when you live an adulterous life be able to maintain your purity of purpose and life's momentum?

51. Your mind will become corrupt and reprobate.

Because that, when they knew God, they glorified him not as God, neither were thankful; but became vain in their imaginations, and their foolish heart was darkened. Professing themselves to be wise, they became fools. And even as they did not like to retain God in their knowledge, God gave them over to a reprobate mind, to do those things which are not convenient (Romans 1:21-22, 28).

Only the light of the Word of God has the ability to renew your mind and transform your life (Romans 12:1-2). Mind renewal is essential lest you become utterly reprobate and corrupt (Ephesians 4:23).

52. As you age you will go through your mid-life crisis alone.

Going through times and seasons of life without anyone nearby to understand and comfort you can be a lonely road. A lifelong companion who fully knows and unconditionally loves you is an invaluable asset. To once have had such a person in your life and then be without such a treasure is a great loss indeed.

53. You'll have nobody to care for you in your old age.

Logistically speaking, once you enter your senior years being without the assistance of your spouse can be physically challenging. Should any unexpected physical ailment, disease, or agedness set in to whom will you turn for assistance? Our bodies weren't made to endure forever. Our nation's young people are becoming increasingly self-centered. Sadly we can't always count on our children to be there for us as they will eventually marry and have lives of their own to live. Assisted living and nursing home care certainly does not come with the tender loving touch that a spouse would give.

54. You'll be assured the judgment of God in this life and in the world to come.

"Whoremongers and adulterers God will judge" (Hebrews 13:4). Beyond the penalty of personal defilement and dishonor, you can rest assured there will be additional consequences with which to attend to both on earth and in heaven hereafter. "For we must all appear before the judgment seat of Christ; that everyone may receive the things done in his body, according to that he has done, whether it be good or bad" (2Corinthians 5:10). God by Christ Jesus will judge the living and the dead (2 Timothy 4:1).

55. Your perspective will be perverted and influence greatly diminished as you go into hiding becoming a recluse and isolating yourself in shame.

"The wages of sin is death" (Romans 6:23a). As in the beginning, sin makes humanity hide in shame. Adam and Eve after sinning against God went into hiding (Genesis 3:7-8). Sin weakens your heart, destroys you within, breeds excessive self-consciousness and causes you to hide in shame to cover yourself. Hence sin perverts your perspective, dwarfs your self-image, and diminishes your influence in society.

56. The fond memories and experiences will not be able to be shared with your beloved spouse with whom you lived and enjoyed them. They will be forever gone.

Marriage is a place where wonderful experiences, delightful interaction, familial bonding and holidays are shared. It is a relationship where your memory bank can be filled with sacred and harmonious experiences which you lived together. Even personal struggles and difficulties endured together, when looked back upon during your lives, become reason for laughter and merriment. To throw all of this marvelous history away for merely momentary gratuitous sex is mindless and meaningless.

57. Sorrow will fill your heart and home.

One particular song says: "No one knows what it's like to be a sad man, to be a mad man, to be hated …behind blue eyes." When you cheat you fill your own heart with self disgust, as you begin to loathe yourself for your vile actions. Your heart will sink to the depths of despair and sorrow will fill your soul. Sorrow spreads once you open the floodgates of sin. Following sin, sorrow does not hesitate to come in. Not only will you experience it as the perpetrator of evil deeds, but your home and family will know it too.

58. Strangers will fondle and hold your beloved.

You always eventually reap in life what you sow. This in time you shall fully know. King David murdered Bathsheba's husband so he could take his wife. God swiftly and progressively judged him for doing so.

God sent the prophet Nathan to rebuke King David. The Lord said to David through His prophet, "Wherefore have you despised the commandment of the Lord, to do evil in His sight? You have killed Uriah the Hittite with the sword, and have taken his wife to be your wife, and have slain him with the sword of the children of Ammon. Now therefore the sword shall never depart from your house; because you despised Me, and have taken the wife of Uriah the Hittite to be your wife." Thus saith the Lord, "Behold, I will raise up evil against you out of your own house, and I will take your wives before your eyes, and give them unto your neighbor, and he shall lie with your wives in the sight of this sun" (2 Samuel 12:9-11)

In despising God's commandments written in His Word, David essentially despised God Himself. Such disregard for the Word of the Lord was swiftly judged by God. Not only did David and Bathsheba's out-of-wedlock child die, but a more severe judgment came upon David. His own son Absalom slept with his father's concubines in broad day light before all of Israel bringing further dishonor upon David (2 Samuel 16:22).

59. Attorneys will seize your assets and take that which is precious to you away in a moment of time.

Divorce lawyers can be very ruthless when it comes to divorce proceedings. They don't do what they do because they want to reconcile your marriage. Thank God for the few attorneys who advise disgruntled spouses to first seek marital counseling to try to reconcile before proceeding with a court case. Make no mistake about it. The majority however are in it for the money. And the more the lawyers can get for their client (a.k.a. your spouse and future ex), they will do so. After all, their compensation often comes proportionately directly out of how much they earn for their client. So dollar signs are in their head as they head to the courthouse.

Is it really worth it to jeopardize all of your lifelong work by which you've accumulated your worldly goods for a cheap thrill? I think not! What you currently may think to be a sexual thrill is nothing more than a poison pill.

60. Your discernment will depart from you after which you will be left to grope in utter darkness.

When you disregard your inner conscience and continually quiet it in favor of your flesh, eventually your guts will go away. That is your conscience will check out since you've repeatedly disregarded its cries from within to save your life. Once seared and swept away by sin, your discernment will be no more. Without discernment your life will swiftly be devastated and brought down leaving you to live in utter darkness.

There is a darkness of the soul that brings great depression and heaviness of heart. It can be felt within and even outwardly visibly seen on a person. Spiritual darkness and heaviness of heart can be seen on a person. When a person loses their integrity, joy, and light in their eyes, life is not worth living.

61. Friendships previously a part of your life will leave as many will no longer want to associate with an unstable person.

Friendships are based on trust and covenant. Be it implied or stated outright, people want to associate with those they can trust. Trust is not blindly given, but it is earned over time. When your life goes awry and all hell is breaking loose, you are not the ideal candidate for winning friends. This is why when adultery occurs, many friends move on and go their separate ways. Your friends spouses won't want them to associate with you, lest you misguide them too.

62. You'll have to tell your relational history to the next woman you date.

Another not so glamorous thing about adultery is it becomes part of your life's history. People talk you know. So eventually you will have to explain to your next future spouse why your last marriage went sour. Such information cannot be hidden forever. It is better to be honest and forthright rather than your next spouse to find it out herself via other sources. And by the way, when a person assesses someone to possibly marry, hearing about your previous infidelity won't make them want to run to the altar with you!

So then why not keep the spouse you've got! Finding a replacement might be harder than you think. Most people don't foresee marrying a divorced person in their love plan. I've never heard of someone dreaming to marry a divorced person. It's rather the opposite as most tend to shy away from and avoid divorcees since they've already failed once at marriage and have a poor track record.

63. You'll have to go to the courthouse and take care of legalities.

Divorce proceedings are no piece of cake. Legalities involved in a divorce proceeding are nerve racking, not to mention mentally and emotionally exhausting. Some people have had to deal with lawyers, judges and extensive legal paperwork for years to get a divorce. Getting rid of a spouse may not be as easy as you think. Furthermore once your loved one becomes your enemy, you may have hell on your hands for quite some time before you can sever the marriage. Is it really worth it to cheat? I think not!

64. You may never find forgiveness and relief for your soul from the spouse you betrayed.

Some people think because their spouse is so loving and because they have kids, that they will find a place of forgiveness for their adulterous behavior. You had better think twice before you jump in the sack with someone else. Because when you get home, your clothes and belongings might be taken out with the trash. Don't prematurely assume forgiveness for unforgivable actions. Adultery is Biblical grounds for divorce, permissible in the eyes of God and man (Matthew 19:9).

65. Feelings of joy and happiness will perish.

Innocence and childlike purity bring about feelings of joy. Inner joy radiates forth when you as a person are congruent in yourself. That means you know who you are, what you are about and have your life's purpose figured out. This is the place of personal passion and optimal performance. Adultery sabotages your soul and thwarts your personal congruency bringing about instability. With such instability will come guilt, shame, double-mindedness and unhappiness.

66. Close your eyes and imagine that cherished spouse forever leaving you – your stomach will ascend to your throat.

Sometimes we need to visualize the worst to appreciate the best. Lest you learn to envision the possible pain from a misstep, you might make it and live it. It can sometimes be beneficial to play out in your mind a course of action to see ultimately where it might take you and assess internally if it is for you. Since men are so visual and can fantasize about women in regard to adulterous affairs, why not visualize the aftermath of the affair and see where it takes you. See yourself getting caught, brought to your knees in utter devastation and ousted from your family on all fours in depravity.

67. Your health will suffer as gall fills your soul and your intestines anguish within.

The wages of sin is death (Rom.6:23a). Make no mistake about it. Sin brings sickness physically (John 5:14). Don't play with sin! It will take you further than you want to go, cost you more than you want to pay and take your dreams away! Sin is the blast that doesn't last! What will last however is your internal woes, indigestion and bodily infirmity.

David, a man after God's own heart, sinned dreadfully after which he suffered immensely physically (Psalm 51:8-9). Sickness is a dose of death that drags on making you sometimes prefer death to put a stop to the pain. Say no to adultery today and put a stop to your pain before it begins or gets any worse than it already is!

68. You may experience the death of a child through fornication. David and Bathsheba lost their first child.

Because of David's disobedience to God, the child he and Bathsheba conceived out of wedlock was not blessed and died. The prophet Nathan foretold this saying to David, "Howbeit, because by this deed you have given great occasion to the enemies of the Lord to blaspheme, the child also that is born unto you shall surely die. And the Lord struck the child that Uriah's wife bare unto David, and it was very sick." (2 Samuel 12:14-15).

God hates divorce and desires a godly seed from holy matrimony (Malachi 2:14-16). The reciprocal is true too. God takes no pleasure in the procreation of the wicked, nor does He want them to fill the earth with their wickedness. The sins of the fathers God will visit down to three and four generations of those that hate Him (Exodus 20:5).

69. Relational walls will be erected within your soul despite the forgiveness God may grant you.

When you commit adultery, inwardly within your soul, walls of distrust are erected. This is so whether you realize it or not because of your own distrust for yourself. Your words suddenly carry less weight and credibility. Hence you are less apt to believe others and take them at their word. It is a known fact psychologically that we often relationally project on others what we perceive about ourselves. "Unto the pure all things are pure: but unto them that are defiled and unbelieving is nothing pure; but even their mind and conscience is defiled" (Titus 1:15).

Walls historically were erected to keep people out. Relationally walls can also be erected by reason of distrust to guard our wounded hearts and protect us. Yet until the hurt within is healed, you will project your hurt onto others and not have wholesome relationships. Adultery is a false relationship pretending to satisfy, when it does nothing of the sort. Whatever things you disclose to the adulteress outside of covenant will assuredly be told to others. When it is all said and done what you have revealed about yourself will be made known to all and your so-called "friend," who you thought so understands you, will turn on you to become a fiend. In the end you will be left to yourself behind walls of distrust. Be vulnerable and open with your spouse, not another outside your house.

70. You won't be able to look your wife in the eyes without your heart condemning you.

Even if you can manage to cheat on your spouse without getting caught, your own heart within will condemn you. "If our heart condemns us, God is greater than our heart, and knows all things" (1 John 3:20). "Happy is he that condemns not himself in that thing which he allows" (Romans 14:22).

If your heart within is condemning you with the weight and guilt of your sin, that is not living the abundant life God has for you. God wants you to be able to look into your spouse's eyes with purity, joy and freedom in your heart. Seducing you into sin and burying you afterward with condemnation is the devil's art.

71. You'll have to live with trying to always cover up your wrongdoing through lies and deception.

One lie leads to another. Telling lies to always cover your tracks can be exhausting. Not to mention it can begin to give you an identity crisis as your mind eventually cannot distinguish between your real life and your false one. Telling a lie kills your conscience. Living a lie kills your personhood. Don't be deceived by observing and following after lying vanities.

72. Everywhere you go they who knew your former spouse will ask about them and you'll have to be the bearer of bad news.

Going out in public while being separated or after a divorce is not a pleasant experience. Everywhere you go and bump into people, they will ask about your spouse. Telling the same old sad story repeatedly can become exhausting. Spare yourself the agony and drama by being faithful.

73. You may never bounce back emotionally from the grief and thereafter live with heaviness of heart all the days of your life.

The grief and agony of adultery is a monumental overload on your emotions. It is such a heavy weight on your soul that you begin to carry this heaviness with you everywhere you go. It slows you down emotionally and mentally, while thwarting your productivity. Getting the bounce back in your step and regaining childlike purity following adultery is very difficult to do. Spare yourself the agony to begin with and don't commit adultery.

74. God's finest choice for your days on earth will be lost and the best you will ever get thereafter is good as best will be forever gone.

Adultery is not God's best. Once you have tarnished your life and personal testimony by adultery, getting back to God's perfect will is nearly impossible. What is best is always most blessed.

Don't throw away that which is best to merely pursue something that is good. There is no good in adultery! And getting back to good after adultery may take years to do. That which is ultimately best may not always feel good momentarily when you are going through difficulty. Nevertheless value and guard that which is best because when it is all said and done it is the road that is most blessed and rewarding.

75. Thoughts of suicide and low self-esteem will bombard your mind.

The devil always preys on the weak. Adultery is a devastating blow to your self-esteem. It is quite common for people to go through suicidal tendencies after an affair as their personhood is heavily questioned and under attack. The depths of guilt and despair can continually haunt you after committing adultery. Sadly some have resorted to terminating their lives to escape such negative personal feedback from their conscience after adultery.

76. Demon spirits will harass and continually remind you of your mistake.

Demon spirits are always looking for an open door to attack humanity and gain entrance to their soul. Disobedience is an open door for the devil to get into your mind and begin to work havoc. Lying spirits full of railing accusations often try to belittle and crush a person following an ungodly sinful act that they know to have been wrong. Don't play with adultery unless you are prepared to entertain and wrestle with demons afterward. Adultery opens the door for the hoards of hell to assault you.

77. Your hopes and dreams formerly expressed with your spouse will at times come to your remembrance at various places and times throughout your life. Yet they will not be there to pursue and enjoy, only there to haunt you as to what could have been.

Hopes and dreams we share and pursue together in marriage are a major part of our life's purpose. Once such destiny determinations are made, the soul stakes claim to them and begins to direct one's life en route to fulfilling them. Adultery is a sudden detour and curve ball that deviates from your life's direction and purpose. After committing adultery, the echoes of previous purposeful conversations will still reverberate and come to memory. The reality however is once the marital relationship has been violated, personal passion and momentum to pursue your deeper purpose will be greatly diminished and dwarfed.

78. Holidays won't be as special without your spouse.

Holidays and family traditions you have grown to love and celebrate will be lost by adultery. Special days will have less meaning as your heart will condemn you. The role your spouse plays in marriage and during the holidays will be dampened. Things done joyously from the heart before with love and service will be no more, as the heart within will depart.

79. Many tears will be shed.
You will cry yourself to sleep with regret. Though you cry incessantly and may find a place of repentance, you will never be able to reverse the wrong you have done. It will forever tarnish the relationship. Crying over something you did that could have been avoided had you heeded others warnings and precautions is grievously painful. Tears alone will never turn the course of events your adultery caused. Great sorrow will fill your heart and tears will assuredly flow like a river.

80. All the people who attended your wedding will come to mind, the images of the wedding ceremony and you'll feel horrible for lying to God and those present.
When you get married in front of family and friends, you vocalized vows and commitments before a sacred assembly. Videotapes with pictures from your wedding will periodically flash back through your mind and haunt you. Such ongoing images will make you feel horrible for what you did and who you are as a person. Adultery comes at a heavy price as it pertains to your internal imagery.

81. Pictures will forever remind you of what once was.

Your memory books and marital keepsakes, such as photos taken and knickknacks collected over the years will be a continual source of remembrance to what you lost because of your adultery. Getting rid of them from your photo albums and computer files will take time to do. This will be another painful, tormenting experience for you.

82. You will have to account for unwritten chapters in your life as the pages of your life will have been ripped out before the Author of life could finish writing His story with you and your wife.

Once you commit adultery, you have to begin deleting pages from your personal account. Removing chapters from your life story can be demoralizing as you try afresh to rewrite the story of your life. Adultery tares and rips the pure and precious life from you. Adultery destroys everything that is intended to be a part of your life's legacy, leaving you to have to start all over from the ground up again.

83. Songs that meant something to you will become sad memories of the past.

Songs that were meaningful to you when married will unexpectedly come on the radio when you are in your car, out dining, or socializing bringing back memories. Those past meaningful moments anchored to those songs will cause you to suddenly feel and relive those emotions. Hence there is no escape, nor return as adultery abandons and strands you in the most precarious place emotionally.

84. Qualities beyond the physical will suddenly come into focus that your spouse has and that often were a blessing to you. Yet it will be a discovery made too late, as they will be gone.

Many times we take for granted our spouse and all the things that make them special. Because our world and media are so heavily fixated on the physical, it is easy to only focus on the outside. Yet once you have severed your marital union by adultery and the spouse you said "I do" to walks out on you, suddenly all of their wonderful inner qualities will be missed and desirable. Don't take for granted a person's inner world and beauty. Before diving into the bed of adultery, consider the inner beauty of your spouse and what that means to you. Inner beauty far outweighs outer beauty in the grand scheme of life. Don't let adultery destroy and steal from you the true riches within.

85. Your level of appreciation for your spouse will increase when they are gone and you realize what a blessing to your life they really were.

Blessings are always appreciated more once they are gone for some reason. It is a pity and tragedy, but human beings appreciate what they don't have more than what they do have.

86. You'll have to eat alone and cook your own dinners.

Eating alone is not always enjoyable. Get used to it though if you plan to be an adulterer, as people will quickly go out of your life.

87. You'll have to schedule visiting hours with the kids and enjoy weekends apart.

Spending time with your kids will have to be scheduled periodically at the permission of your ex. It is amazing how quickly you can lose your children after a divorce. Having to fight for visitation rights in court and enduring scheduling time between your former spouse to see your kids is tough. Ask Alec Baldwin. Consider how troubling it will be for both you and your children to have to live with your ex-wife's new lover? Do you really want to subject yourself and your children to living with an absolute stranger?

88. You'll have to clean the house by yourself.

Being single again means you will be doing all the household chores and duties alone. A helping hand removed is often more appreciated in its absence. Don't take your precious spouse for granted and all they do for you.

89. Your home will revert to a house without your spouse.

Without the presence of your spouse, your home will merely be a house. That loving feeling and homey atmosphere created by two people living together in heartfelt love will be gone. Love's harmonious flow and rhythm will be lost. Without the intangible aspects of your love, your home will simply be concrete, wood and walls.

90. That which you have together accumulated and produced will suddenly decrease in value.

The efforts of two by far exceed the ability of one alone. Combined efforts always lead to exponential results. Marriage puts in motion the multiplication factor. Divorce sets in motion the division variable which rapidly reduces and devalues.

91. You'll reap disrespect and dishonesty for that which you've sown.

The disregard, disrespect and dishonesty you show to your present spouse will always boomerang back to you over the course of time. Undoubtedly what you sow, you do truly reap. The law of reciprocity is an inescapable universal truth.

92. An orgasm only lasts a short time anyway, but a marriage can last a lifetime.

Love endures and lasts a lifetime. An orgasm and sexual fling only lasts a short time. It is not worth throwing away your marriage for a miniscule momentary thrill. Before you do something you later will regret, take a cold shower and just chill.

93. You will grow old alone.

Keep things in perspective. When you're old and a senior citizen you might not be able to get it up anyhow. So why not guard your marital relationship now? It may be all you've got in your old age.

Apart from viagra, many men won't be able to function sexually in their later years. It may be Niagra now, but in your old age you may be sluggish as a cow. Therefore don't underestimate the importance of inner qualities that are valuable in every season of your life. Growing old alone is very undesirable.

94. You will die miserable and alone.

Eventually we're all going to get old and die. What do you want to be remembered for? Being a perverted sex crazed man?

The way you handle your marriage will be a significant part of your life legacy. Do you want your legacy to be marred by bad behavior and unfaithfulness? Do you want to be known throughout town as a pervert who can't keep his pants on? Consider your ways and be mindful of your reputation. God says in his Word that your name is worth more than riches (Proverbs 22:1).

95. When you sleep around you leave a piece of yourself everywhere you go and eventually you'll not know who you are anymore.

Adultery divides your soul and thwarts your mental sense of security causing you to be double-minded and unstable in all your ways (James 1:8).

96. Adulterers go to the lake of fire.

The sexually immoral will burn for eternity in the lake of fire reserved for the devil and the disobedient who shunned God's commandments (Rev.21:8).

97. Flattery works ruin.

A flattering mouth works ruin. (Prov.26:28) The devil is great at telling lies (John 10:10). He was a liar from the beginning and is the father of lies (John 8:44). Don't believe any person willing to commit adultery with you. If they will commit adultery with you, they also will commit adultery against you. Adultery is swiftly followed by calamity.

98. Sin causes you to hide and run from God.

Adam and Eve went into hiding in Eden after they sinned (Genesis 3:7-9). Their disobedience caused the covering of God's glory to be removed from them, after which they tried to sew together some fig leaves to cover themselves.

99. Spiritual and gross darkness will weigh heavily upon you.

The darkness of sin is so gross it often can be felt (Exodus 10:21). The wicked shall dwell in the mist of darkness for eternity as punishment for their wrongdoing (2 Peter 2:4,17). Perversity is a breach in the spirit. Perversity breaks and crushes your spirit within (Proverbs 15:4). Your innermost life in the spirit will be snuffed out by adultery.

100. "It's not easy being single."

While I was living and working in California at the Hyatt hotel, I overheard a lady comment on her life as a single woman. She had been attending a singles event there and was leaving at the conclusion of the function. As she waited for the valet to pull up her car, she said: "I should have never divorced my husband. It's not easy being single."

Cultivate an attitude of gratitude for your spouse. Love them. Serve them. Be attentive to their needs. It is more blessed to give than receive (Acts 20:35). Let go of that offense and root of bitterness. Be the person God intended for you to be. Uphold your marital vows and you will be blessed beyond your wildest dreams, as you press into know and obey God. Everything of any value in this life is worth fighting for. Undoubtedly your marriage is of highest value and worthy of working to improve. I pray God's greatest blessing on you as you do.

Hold on to God's unchanging hand and He'll see you through what you're going through.

Currently you may feel overwhelmed, bitter, emboldened and ready to go to battle. Nevertheless don't move hastily and respond negatively. Be proactive and precautious before making any missteps. Hold on to God tightly and seek His wisdom in regard to every step you make during this crucial time.

The Savior loves us despite us. His commitment to unconditionally love humanity is unchanging. God is first and foremost faithful to His Word and therefore cannot deny Himself. When we remain faithful to our word to our spouse, it shows the world the extent of God's love and commitment toward them.

Exemplify Christ's unconditional love and commitment to the world. Your life speaks louder than words. When you refuse to be a playboy and remain committed to your wife, it signifies to the world the steadfast love of God. As the sun rises every morning without fail, the Son of God's love is over the just and the evil. Even when we do wrong and are unfaithful, God remains steadfast and faithful toward us.

101. The curse shall devour you.

When you disobey God and refuse to hearken to His commandments, many curses will come upon you and overtake you (see Deut.28:15-68). You shall be smitten before your enemies (v.25). You shall grope about as a blind man and not prosper in your ways (v. 29).

Your sons and daughters shall go into captivity (Deuteronomy 28:41). When the parents eat sour grapes, the children's teeth are set on edge (Ezekiel 18:2). Walk uprightly considering your ways, lest your seed be made to suffer generationally for your disregard (Exodus 20:5-6).

We are living in a day of gross darkness as ungodliness abounds in North America. Nevertheless the light of God shall arise upon His people and His glory shall be seen in His church (Isaiah 60:1-2).

"The earth mourns and fades away, the world languishes and fades away, the haughty people of the earth do languish. The earth also is defiled under the inhabitants thereof; because they have transgressed the laws, changed the ordinance, broken the everlasting covenant. Therefore hath the curse devoured the earth, and they that dwell therein are desolate (Isaiah 24:4-6).

Prayer of Repentance and Restoration

There is forgiveness with God, that He may be feared (Psalm 130:4).

Whether you have committed adultery or been victimized by it, you must know that your Father in heaven loves and is fighting for you. Nothing can separate you from the love of God – nothing you have done, no matter how vile or gross.

Pray this prayer out loud with your voice to God in heaven now!

"Dear Jesus, thank You for dying for me and my sins. Please forgive me for things I have said and done in violation of your Word and ways. Holy Jesus, please cleanse me from my sins by Your blood that You shed for me on the cross. Righteous Lord, please send Your Holy Spirit to live big in me and make my life what it ought to be. I surrender my life to You now Jesus. As you rose from the dead, please come to transform and resurrect my life. Liberate me from myself and create a new heart within me. Come Holy Spirit and live in me. Purify and prepare me for marriage. Deliver me from evil. Lead me in the way of truth and righteousness. Turn darkness into light; death into life; cursing into blessing; and evil into good. Almighty God, turn me and my situation around. Let your love and mercy to me now abound. In Jesus Name I pray. Amen."

If you prayed that prayer sincerely from your heart, I would like to hear from you. Please write me at RevivingNations@yahoo.com or send a letter to Dream-Maker Ministries, PO Box 684, Goldenrod, FL 32733 USA.

There is therefore now no condemnation to them who are in Christ Jesus, who walk not after the flesh, but after the Spirit. For the law of the Spirit of life in Christ Jesus has made me free from the law of sin and death (Romans 8:1-2).

The blood of Christ, through the eternal Spirit, will purge your conscience from dead works to serve the living God (Hebrews 9:14).

For I will be merciful to their unrighteousness, and their sins and their iniquities will I remember no more (Hebrews 8:12).

And their sins and iniquities will I remember no more (Hebrews 10:17).

I beseech you therefore, brethren, by the mercies of God, that ye present your bodies a living sacrifice, holy, acceptable unto God, which is your reasonable service. And be not conformed to this world: but be transformed by the renewing of your mind, that you may prove what is that good, and acceptable, and perfect, will of God (Romans 12:1-2).

For they that are after the flesh do mind the things of the flesh; but they that are after the Spirit the things of the Spirit. For to be carnally minded is death; but to be spiritually minded is life and peace. Because the carnal mind is enmity against God: for it is not subject to the law of God, neither indeed can be (Romans 8:5-7).

For if you live after the flesh, you shall die: but if you through the Spirit do mortify the deeds of the body, you shall live (Romans 8:13).

Not by might, nor by power, but by My Spirit, saith the Lord of hosts (Zechariah 4:6).

It is through the help of the Holy Spirit that you will overcome the lusts of flesh, not in your own strength. Read my book *Stop Lusting & Start Living: A Sexual Recovery Plan.*

Likewise the Spirit also helps our infirmities: for we know not what we should pray for as we ought: but the Spirit itself makes intercession for us with groanings which cannot be uttered. And He that searches the hearts knows what is the mind of the Spirit, because He makes intercession for the saints according to the will of God (Romans 8:26-27).

And we know that all things work together for good to them that love God, to them who are the called according to his purpose (Romans 8:28).

What shall we then say to these things? If God be for us, who can be against us? He that spared not his own Son, but delivered him up for us all, how shall He not with Him also freely give us all things? (Romans 8:31-32)

Who shall separate us from the love of Christ? Shall tribulation, or distress, or persecution, or famine, or nakedness, or peril, or sword? (Romans 8:35)

No, in all these things we are more than conquerors through Him that loved us. For I am persuaded, that neither death, nor life, nor angels, nor principalities, nor powers, nor things present, nor things to come, nor height, nor depth, nor any other creature, shall be able to separate us from the love of God, which is in Christ Jesus our Lord (Romans 8:37-39).

God's love for humanity is steadfast and unconditional. The blessing of the Lord however is conditional upon our obedience.

He will fulfill the desire of them that fear him: He also will hear their cry, and will save them (Psalm 145:19).

The Lord takes pleasure in them that fear him, in those that hope in His mercy (Psalm 147:11).

Fear the Lord and Depart from Evil

Wrongdoing is always followed by the consequences of our actions. This has nothing to do with the Creator and everything to do with us. Often we afflict ourselves by reason of our own wrongdoing.

When we learn obedience to God's Word, it is well with us. Sadly our modern culture and legal system has fought God in such a way that His commandments and Word has been removed from society to the extent that we don't know it anymore.

This is why children are killing in the public schools. Since the 10 Commandments have been removed from the schools, the school ground has been turned into a battleground. "Thou shall not kill" is no longer seen or heard in schools. When the United States public schools began, the first book used for education was the Holy Bible. The Word of God gives to humanity commandments, borders within which to live, to advance and protect our lives.

When God's judgments are in the earth, the inhabitants of the world will learn righteousness (Isaiah 26:9).

Before I [David] was afflicted I went astray: but now have I kept Your Word (Psalm 119:67).

It is good for me that I have been afflicted; that I might learn Your statutes (Psalm 119:71).

I know, O LORD, that Your judgments are right, and that You in faithfulness have afflicted me (Psalm 119:75).

The fear of the LORD is clean, enduring forever: the judgments of the LORD are true and righteous altogether (Psalm 19:9).

He is the LORD our God: His judgments are in all the earth (Psalm 105:7).

Turn away my reproach which I fear: for Your judgments are good (Psalm 119:39).

Great are Your tender mercies, O Lord: quicken me according to Your judgments (Psalm 119:156).

Your Word is true from the beginning: and every one of Your righteous judgments endures for ever (Psalm 119:160).

The fear of the Lord is the beginning of knowledge and wisdom (Proverbs 1:7; 9:10).

The fear of the Lord is to hate evil (Proverbs 8:13).

The fear of the Lord prolongs days: but the years of the wicked shall be shortened (Proverbs 10:27).

A wise man fears, and departs from evil (Proverbs 14:16).

The fear of the Lord is a fountain of life, to depart from the snares of death (Proverbs 14:27).

By humility and the fear of the Lord are riches, and honor, and life (Proverbs 22:4).

The fear of the Lord is clean, enduring for ever: the judgments of the Lord are true and righteous altogether (Psalm 19:9).

The angel of the Lord encamps round about them that fear him, and delivers them (Psalm 34:7).

O fear the Lord, you His saints: for there is no want to them that fear Him (Psalm 34:9).

For as the heaven is high above the earth, so great is His mercy toward them that fear Him (Psalm 103:11).

Like as a father pities his children, so the LORD pities them that fear Him (Ps.103:13).

He hath given meat unto them that fear Him: he will ever be mindful of His covenant (Psalm 111:5).

The mercy of the Lord is from everlasting to everlasting upon them that fear Him, and His righteousness with their children's children (Ps.103:17).

Blessed is every one that fears the Lord; that walks in His ways (Ps.128:1).

Behold, thus shall the man be blessed that fears the Lord (Psalm 128:4).

For the Lord is great, and greatly to be praised: He is to be feared above all gods (Psalm 96:4).

About the Author

Paul Davis is a worldwide professional speaker, life coach, and minister empowering people to live their dreams. A master in the art of communication and neurolinguistic programming, Paul has received extensive academic training and spiritual impartation from the best and the brightest. A highly sought after professional speaker, Paul's messages inspire, revive, awaken, impregnate with purpose, impart the fire of desire, catapult people into a new level of self-awareness, facilitate destiny discovery and dream fulfillment.

Paul has served many from working at ground zero during 911, serving in impoverished and tsunami stricken regions of the earth, and addressing audiences in war-torn nations. A minister of love, wisdom and power to the peoples of the world, Paul Davis breaks the mold, builds the individual, co-creates with you a compelling future to catapult you forward, enabling you to discover your intended destiny and fulfill your lifelong dreams!

Paul is a masterful poet and prolific author of several books including his pre-911 book *A State of*

Emergency; *Breakthrough for a Broken Heart*; *Waves of God*; *Stop Lusting & Start Living*; Supernatural *Fire*; *Are You Ready for True Love?*; Poems That Propel the Planet; *Almighty Matchmaker* and many more!

Paul is a brilliant innovator, visual demonstrator and ingenious communicator. Paul possesses an uncanny ability to get beneath the layers of deception and denial, address the root problems inherent within an individual or organization while altering their perception, reconstructing their reality, renewing their vitality and moving them forth unto fulfilling their destiny.

Academically outstanding, Paul has collected degrees and certificates of completion from the University of Central Florida, Spirit Life Bible College, U. of Washington, Harvard Business School, Hofstra Law School, Hong Kong Law School and Reid & Associates in Advanced Interrogation. He is also Master Practitioner in NLP and Human Design Engineering. Paul excels in Communication, Negotiation, Transformative Mediation (Conflict Resolution), Counseling and Coaching. A Certified Fitness Trainer, Life Coach, and Licensed Minister — Paul is well equipped to fully develop a person's spirit, soul and body.

If you have unfulfilled dreams and longings of the heart that have yet to be realized, let Paul help you to pierce through your self-imposed limitations, pioneer a new path and passionately go after your dreams with a ferocious unstoppable passion! Bold and fearless, Paul has risked his own life for the results he has produced in the lives of others. Paul has defied natural law going to war-torn countries and nations on the brink of destruction to deliver his message. Indeed this man is the message.

Paul & Karla Davis can be contacted for Professional Speaking, Consulting, Coaching (professional & relational), Conflict Resolution, Restoring Order (professional organizing) and much more!

Paul & Karla Davis
Dream-Maker Inc.
PO Box 684
Goldenrod, FL 32733 USA
407-284-1705; 407-967-7553
RevivingNations@yahoo.com
www.DreamMakerMinistries.com
www.CreativeCommunications.TV
www.PaulnKarla.com
www.itietheknot.com

www.ingramcontent.com/pod-product-compliance
Ingram Content Group UK Ltd.
Pitfield, Milton Keynes, MK11 3LW, UK
UKHW041943230426
12048UKWH00008B/106